CENTRAL AFRICA

NICOLA BARBER

UGA

ANDA

BURUM

CRATIC
OF CON

ZAM

W
FRANKLIN WATTS
LONDON•SYDNEY

Designer Steve Prosser
Editor Simon Adams
Art Director Jonathan Hair
Editor-in-Chief John C. Miles
Picture Research Diana Morris
Map artwork Ian Thompson

© 2005 Franklin Watts

First published in 2005
by Franklin Watts
96 Leonard Street
London
EC2A 4XD

Franklin Watts Australia
45-51 Huntley Street
Alexandria
NSW 2015

ISBN 0 7496 5543 7

A CIP catalogue record for this book is
available from the British Library.

Printed in Malaysia

Picture credits
AP/Topham: 26
Bettman/Corbis: 16
Adil Bradlow/Trace Images/Topham: front
cover top, 36
British Library/HIP/Topham: 12
EPA/PA: 31
Louise Gubb/Image Works/Topham: 37
Hulton Deutsch/Corbis: 10b, 19
Image Works/Topham: back cover, 39
Szenes Jason/Sygma/Corbis: front cover below,
29b
Richard Lord/Image Works/Topham: 41
PA/Topham: 33.
Picturepoint/Topham: 8, 14, 15, 17, 18, 20, 32
Popperfoto: 21
Reuters/Corbis: 27
Patrick Robert/Sygma/Corbis: 30
Tim Rooke/Rex Features: 40
Sipa/Rex Features: 22, 23, 25, 35
Allan Tannebaum/Image Works/Topham: 29t
Topham: 11t
UPP/Topham: 24, 34, 38

*Every attempt has been made to clear copyright.
Should there be any inadvertent omission
please apply to the publisher for rectification.*

CONTENTS

INTRODUCTION

Central Africa is a vast region that extends south from the fringes of the Sahara. It is bordered to the west by the Atlantic Ocean and to the east by the Indian Ocean.

THE RIVER CONGO

Geographically, Central Africa is very varied. In the west, the River Congo (once the Zaire) rises in southern Congo and flows in a wide arc north and west before reaching the sea. At 4,670 kilometres, it is the second longest river in Africa, after the Nile. The Congo drains a large area of tropical rainforest. This area has a hot, wet climate all year round. South of the Congo basin lies an area of savannah grassland. This rolling landscape has a tropical climate with wet and dry seasons.

THE GREAT RIFT VALLEY

East of the Congo basin runs the Great Rift Valley, formed by movements in the Earth's crust that have caused deep, parallel cracks in the land. The Great Rift Valley starts in Syria and extends 7,200 kilometres south through Africa to Mozambique. The valley

BANTU

The peoples of Central Africa speak many different languages, which are all related to each other. Bantu, the name given to this family of over 500 languages, is thought to have evolved from a language originally spoken in the region of present-day Cameroon. Some of the main Bantu languages spoken in Central Africa include Swahili, Kongo, Rwanda and Makua.

is between 30 and 100 kilometres wide, with sides rising up to 2,000 metres in places. South of Kenya, the valley splits in two: the western branch forms the eastern border of the Congo, while the eastern branch runs through Kenya and Tanzania. The two branches join again at Lake Nyasa.

East of the Great Rift Valley lie the Eastern Highlands. This grassland region provides grazing for domesticated herds and wild animals. A lowland area of coastal swamp, farmland and long, sandy beaches lies along the East African coast.

TEN FLASHPOINTS

Politically, most countries in this region obtained their independence from European rule during the 1960s. Since then, some have been largely peaceful, while others have acquired a reputation for violence, terror, and misrule. This book examines the recent history of ten of these troubled flashpoints.

The Great Rift Valley in East Africa.

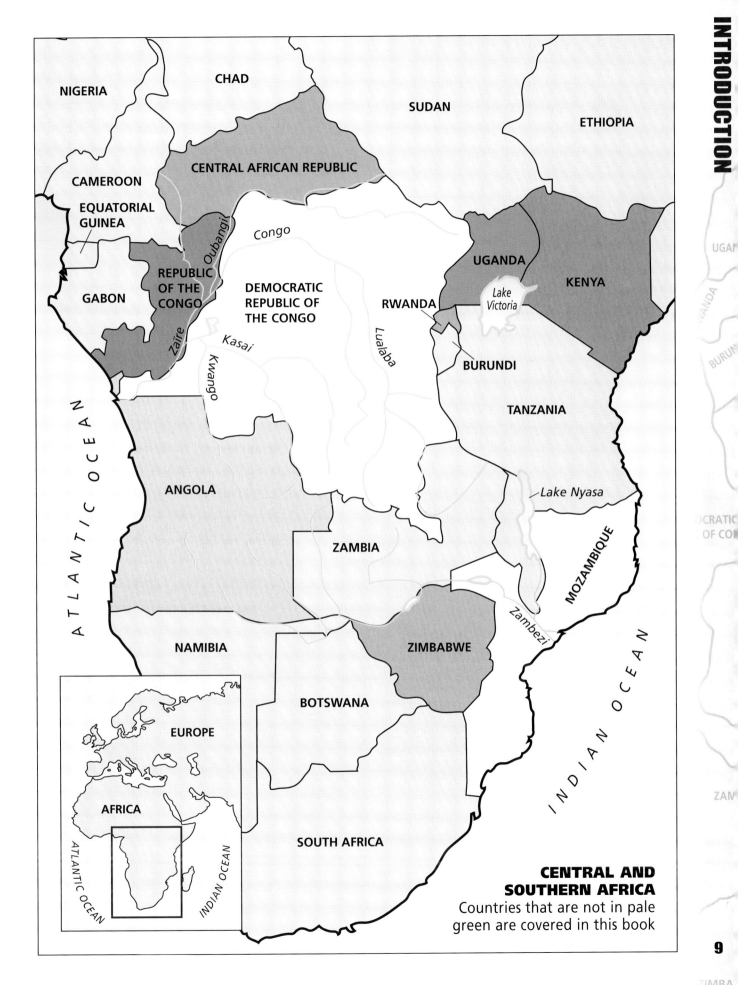

NIGERIA

CHAD

SUDAN

ETHIOPIA

CENTRAL AFRICAN REPUBLIC

CAMEROON

EQUATORIAL
GUINEA

Oubangi

Congo

UGANDA

KENYA

REPUBLIC
OF THE
CONGO

DEMOCRATIC
REPUBLIC OF
THE CONGO

Lake
Victoria

RWANDA

GABON

Zaïre

Kasai

Lualaba

BURUNDI

Kwango

TANZANIA

ATLANTIC OCEAN

ANGOLA

Lake Nyasa

MOZAMBIQUE

ZAMBIA

Zambezi

NAMIBIA

ZIMBABWE

INDIAN OCEAN

EUROPE

BOTSWANA

AFRICA

ATLANTIC OCEAN

INDIAN OCEAN

SOUTH AFRICA

**CENTRAL AND
SOUTHERN AFRICA**
Countries that are not in pale
green are covered in this book

UGAN

WANDA

BURUN

CRATIC
OF CO

ZAM

ZIMBA

EARLY HISTORY

Africa has been called the 'cradle of humankind', for it is here that evidence has been found of the earliest human evolution. The first Stone Age Africans made simple tools for cutting and chopping. They later developed axes, scrapers and arrows.

AGRICULTURE

Early humans lived by hunting wild animals and gathering plants that grew naturally around them. In some places the most plentiful food was found in the local rivers and lakes. Here, fishing communities developed, whose members made harpoon heads and fishhooks from bone, and cooked fish and other foods in simple earthen pots.

The early development of agriculture in Central Africa was probably driven by a change in climate. Between about 8000 and 4000 BC, the climate in the Sahara region was much wetter than it is today and fishing communities became established along the southern fringes of this region. As the climate became drier and the rivers and lakes began to disappear, people living on these southern fringes began to domesticate wild cereal grasses by collecting their seeds and then planting and harvesting them regularly. The most important of these crops were sorghum and millet. In the forest regions of Central Africa, the yam was also domesticated. This activity led to the development of small, settled communities. As the food supply became more regular, the population began to increase.

People also learned to domesticate wild animals such as cattle, sheep and goats, and to live off the milk from these animals. Cattle-keeping became an important way of life in the central Sahara but, as the climate became drier, the cattle-herders gradually moved southwards. However, the spread of pastoralism, as animal herding is called, was affected by a blood-sucking insect called the tsetse fly. A parasite in the saliva of the fly causes sleeping sickness, a disease that can be fatal to both cattle and humans. Tsetse flies are found in wooded and low-lying regions, so pastoralism flourished away from these areas in the drier savannah lands.

BANTU-SPEAKERS

From about 1000 BC, Bantu-speakers began to spread southwards, a movement that was to continue for many centuries until most of sub-Saharan Africa was populated by Bantu-speakers. They also took with them a knowledge of iron-working, allowing them to produce metal objects, tools and jewellery.

The modern Khoikhoi people of south Central Africa are descendants of the first Bantu speakers.

GREAT ZIMBABWE

Modern-day Zimbabwe (see pages 38–39) takes its name from the kingdom of Great Zimbabwe, which flourished from about 1200 to 1450. The Shona people of Great Zimbabwe were farmers who kept cattle and grew crops. *Zimbabwe* is a Shona word for 'building in stone': the Shona stonemasons used their great skill to build dry-stone walls to create cattle pens, terraced hillsides for crops, and elaborate enclosures for important buildings. Great Zimbabwe was very wealthy, as it controlled the trade between the rich goldfields to its west and the port of Sofala to its east. Great Zimbabwe was abandoned in the 15th century, but the new kingdom of Mutapa soon replaced it.

As the Iron Age began, a new food, the banana, was introduced into East Africa, probably from Southeast Asia, and soon became a staple crop for farmers.

EARLY KINGDOMS

By the later Iron Age (after AD 1000), Central Africa was a region of small communities, many with their own specialities such as food production, fishing, copper-mining or salt manufacture. Along the east coast, the Islamic religion had arrived with Muslim Arab merchants during the 8th century AD. City-states such as Kilwa, Mogadishu and Sofala grew up along the coast on the wealth obtained from trade in gold and ivory, which was brought from

The ruined walls of Great Zimbabwe demonstrate the great skill of Shona stonemasons.

the African interior and taken by Arab and Indian traders to Egypt, Arabia and India.

As trade developed and the population grew, chiefs and kings extended their power. Early kingdoms included those of the Luba around Lake Kisale, and the Luanda kingdom to its west. In west Central Africa, the kingdom of Kongo grew in importance from around 1400, based on trade in raffia textiles.

EARLY HISTORY

c2 million years ago (mya) Early Stone Age in Africa; ancestors of modern humans make simple stone tools	**c40,000 years ago** Late Stone Age in Africa; development of tiny stone blades and a wider range of tools	**c1000 BC** Spread of Bantu-speaking peoples; start of Iron Age in Central Africa	**c1300** Rise of the Luba kingdom
c150,000 years ago Middle Stone Age in Africa; early *Homo sapiens* make more refined tools from stone and bone	**c8000–4000 BC** Last major wet period in the Sahara region	**cAD 1000** Start of the Later Iron Age in Central Africa	**c1400** Rise of the kingdom of Kongo in Congo basin
	c7000 BC First pottery made in Africa	**c1200–1450** Kingdom of Great Zimbabwe flourishes	**c1420** Founding of the Mutapa kingdom
			c1450 Founding of the Luanda kingdom

THE ARRIVAL OF THE EUROPEANS

In the 1480s Portuguese sailors arrived off the coast of western Central Africa. They established relations with the kingdom of Kongo and claimed the uninhabited islands of São Tomé and Príncipe off the coast of modern-day Gabon.

A Portuguese fort on the Kongo coast, used as a collection post for captives shipped into slavery.

THE SLAVE TRADE

The Portuguese established sugar cane plantations on both islands, managed by Portuguese settlers with a slave workforce. These slaves came from the African mainland, supplied by the kingdom of Kongo.

From the 1530s, ships laden with slaves from Central Africa began to sail from the transit port of São Tomé across the Atlantic Ocean to the New World. Here the slaves worked on plantations, mainly in Brazil, which had been claimed by Portugal in 1500. The number of slaves taken across the Atlantic remained relatively small during the 16th century, probably a few thousand each year. However, during the 17th century, the Dutch, followed by the French and British, became involved in the trade and numbers rose dramatically. New ports, such as Luanda and Benguela, joined in the trade.

THE EFFECTS OF SLAVERY

European settlers did not penetrate far inland from the coast, but the effects of the slave trade were felt deep in the interior. Slaves were often prisoners of war, so power

BETWEEN THE LAKES

Several distinct kingdoms arose in the region between Lakes Victoria and Tanganyika. The kingdom of Buganda was based on agriculture, mainly bananas. Buganda dominated the region throughout the 18th and 19th centuries.

To the south of Buganda lay the highland kingdoms of Ruanda and Urundi (or Rundi), roughly modern-day Rwanda and Burundi. In this area lived two main ethnic groups: Tutsi pastoralists and Hutu farmers. The two peoples shared a common language and culture and lived in relative peace until colonial administrations began to favour one group over the other (see pages 28-31), causing resentment and hatred to grow.

struggles between states fed the increasing demand for them. The Europeans wanted strong workers for their plantations; the resulting export of young men from Africa left many societies with an imbalance between their male and female populations.

To pay for slaves, Europeans imported guns and gunpowder, Brazilian rum, wool and cotton cloth. The Europeans also brought new crops from the Americas, including maize, cassava, tobacco, beans and groundnuts. Cassava was particularly important, and soon became a staple crop for the Luanda, Luba and Kazembe kingdoms in the 18th century.

THE EAST COAST

Portuguese sailors reached the east coast of Africa in 1498. During the next century, the Portuguese attacked the various city-states in an attempt to gain a foothold along the coast. They established bases at Kilwa, Sofala, Mozambique and Mombasa, and tried to conquer Mutapa, which controlled the trade in gold (see page 11). Although unsuccessful, they did weaken Mutapa authority.

From the 1630s, Portuguese settlers established landholdings in the Zambezi valley. But in the late 17th century, Changamire, a wealthy cattle-owner, used his trained army − the *Rozvi* ('destroyers') − to set up a kingdom on the Zimbabwe plateau. He restricted the Portuguese to their landholdings and prevented them from taking part in the gold trade.

> '*From our ships the fine houses, terraces and minarets, with the palms and trees in the orchards, made the city look so beautiful that our men were eager to land and overcome the pride of this barbarian.*'
>
> Portuguese eyewitness account of the city of Kilwa, before it was sacked in 1505

THE ARRIVAL OF THE EUROPEANS

1480s Portuguese sailors arrive off west coast of Central Africa	**1498** Portuguese sailors reach the east coast of Africa
1490s Sugar plantations established on São Tomé and Príncipe	**1503** Portuguese attack island of Zanzibar
	1505 Portuguese attack Kilwa, Mombasa and Barawa
1492 Columbus sails to the New World, later named America	

1506 Christian convert seizes throne of Kongo as Afonso I	**c1608** Imported cassava and tobacco crops grown on West African coast
1532 First African captives transported across Atlantic and sold as slaves	**1620s** Mutapa Empire weakens
1599 Completion of Portuguese Fort Jesus at Mombasa	**1680s–90s** Changamire suppresses Portuguese in East Africa

UGAN

ANDA

BURUN

CRATIC
OF CON

AM

13

SLAVES AND MISSIONARIES

By the 19th century, the frontier of the slave trade had pushed far inland, often along river trading routes. The trade in slaves caused massive disruption as some people fought for access to the trade routes while others moved away in search of safety.

SLAVES FOR TRADE

By the end of the 18th century, Britain had become the biggest exporter of slaves from Africa. This changed in 1807, when Britain abolished the slave trade (slavery itself was abolished in 1834). Britain attempted to prevent other countries from exporting slaves by sending naval ships to patrol the West African coast. Nevertheless, the slave trade from Central Africa to Brazil and Cuba continued unabated during the early decades of the 19th century, only coming to an end after 1850. Within Africa, however, the trade did not die out. Slave labour in Central Africa increased, as slaves were put to work to produce food and new goods for export.

The commercial trade that replaced the export of slaves involved three main products: beeswax; ivory from African elephants, used for piano keys, billiard balls, cutlery handles and ornaments; and, later in the century, rubber. Other products grown and processed for export included tobacco, sugar, coffee and palm oil.

Different tribes became important in this trade. The Chokwe hunters of the remote highland regions of Angola used their skills to become specialised ivory hunters and beeswax collectors. When supplies of ivory dried up as the elephants were exterminated, the Chokwe turned their attention to rubber.

MISSIONARIES & EXPLORERS

Many factors led to the British abolition of the slave trade, not least the fact that it was becoming less profitable. The campaign for abolition was closely linked to the growth of the evangelical Christian movement, whose main purpose was to spread Christianity. Large numbers of Christian missionaries went to Africa in the 19th century. Many attempted to establish 'Christianity and commerce' in place of the slave trade. Explorers also played a role in opening up the continent. Men such as Richard Burton, John Speke, James Grant, David Livingstone and Henry Stanley set out to explore the rivers that flowed from the African interior, still largely unknown to Europeans. Information from their travels was vital for the opening up of Africa to increased European commercial exploitation.

David Livingstone (1813–73), Scottish explorer

THE EAST COAST

On the east coast of Africa, the slave trade was small-scale and local until the mid-1700s. Later, however, several factors led to a vast increase in the trade. French colonisers established sugar and coffee plantations on their Indian Ocean colonies of Mauritius and Réunion and imported slaves for these plantations from East Africa. With restrictions on the west-coast slave trade, Brazilian traders also turned their attentions to the east coast. This trade reached its peak in the 1860s before dying out.

The slave trade on the east coast went hand-in-hand with the trade in ivory, which also

The trade in elephant tusks for ivory went hand-in-hand with the slave trade in East Africa.

reached a peak in the late 19th century. The main markets for east-coast ivory had been China and India, but during the 19th century most ivory went to Europe. As the herds of elephants near the coast were killed off, the ivory trade moved further inland. The main suppliers of ivory included the Yao and the Ngoni people north of the Zambezi River, and the Nyamwezi further north again. Raids for ivory and slaves devastated local farming communities and brought chaos to many previously prosperous and peaceful regions.

<table>
<tr><td></td><td>1788 African Association formed in London to promote exploration in Africa</td><td>1814 Holland abolishes slave trade, followed by France in 1817</td><td>c1850 End of export of slaves from Central Africa to Brazil and Cuba</td><td>1865 Slavery abolished in USA</td></tr>
<tr><td rowspan="2">SLAVES AND MISSIONARIES</td><td>1807 Britain abolishes the slave trade</td><td>1834 Slavery abolished in British colonies</td><td>1860 Slavery abolished in Cuba</td><td>1870s–80s Chokwe turn from ivory to rubber production

1873 Slave market in Zanzibar closes</td></tr>
<tr><td>1808 USA abolishes slave trade</td><td>1848 Slavery abolished in French colonies</td><td>1860s Slave trade reaches its peak on east coast of Africa</td><td>1888 Slavery abolished in Brazil</td></tr>
</table>

SCRAMBLE FOR EMPIRES

Between 1880 and 1900, a great change occurred in African history as the European powers partitioned, or divided up, the entire continent between them. Britain, France, Germany, Belgium and Portugal all scrambled to lay claim to Central Africa.

THE BERLIN CONFERENCE

In 1884 the European powers held a conference in Berlin to try to reach some kind of agreement over Africa. The conference was an entirely European affair: no African leaders were present.

The 'scramble for Africa' was in fact well underway by the time of the conference. One of the events that had helped set it off was the interest of the Belgian king, Leopold II, in the activities of the explorer Henry Stanley. On a journey that lasted from 1874 to 1877, Stanley crossed Africa from east to west, making his way down the Congo River to the coast and revealing to the wider world the vast navigable waterway that led into the interior of Central Africa. Leopold sent Stanley back to the Congo in 1879 to oversee the construction of a road around the treacherous rapids on the river. In 1885 Leopold declared a large region south of the River Congo to be the Congo Free State, in effect his own personal kingdom.

In this fanciful painting, Henry Stanley is seen 'cutting his way through the dark continent'.

The serpent Leopold II of Belgium crushes the people of the Congo, as seen in a 19th-century cartoon.

SALVATION AND LIBERATION

The spread of European colonialism in Africa coincided with the development of independent African churches. The impact of colonialism had weakened the authority of local religions, and many young Africans in particular turned to Christianity instead. Christian missions were often the only places that gave access to basic education and healthcare. Some African Christians rebelled against European domination and formed their own independent churches. One example was the Watchtower movement, introduced into Nyasaland (present-day Malawi) by Elliot Kamwana in 1908-09. It preached the second coming of Christ, a time when Africa would be liberated from colonial rule. Another Christian convert was John Chilembwe, who campaigned for equal rights for Africans and who was killed after leading an uprising against colonial injustice.

RIVAL CLAIMS

Stanley was not alone in the Congo. In 1880 the French explorer Savorgnan de Brazza made a treaty with Chief Makoko of the Bateke for land north of the River Congo. Using this and other treaties, France laid claim to Gabon, 'Middle' Congo and Ubangi-Chari (modern-day Central African Republic). Meanwhile, the Portuguese had ancient claims on Central Africa and could not afford to lose out in the scramble for colonies. Portugal was forced to give up any claim to the region around the Congo, but it established colonies in Angola on the west coast and Mozambique on the east.

Both Britain and Germany claimed lands in East Africa. Treaties between the two gave modern-day Kenya and Uganda to Britain and Tanganyika (modern-day Tanzania) to Germany. Both constructed railways into their new colonies, but encountered fierce resistance to their rule. Guerrilla attacks against the British were carried out by the Nandi and the Mazrui in Kenya, while the Germans faced widespread resistance in the early 1900s from the Maji-maji rebellion.

EMPIRE BUILDING

1874–77 Stanley crosses Africa from east to west

1879 Stanley returns to Africa as agent of Leopold II of Belgium

1880 De Brazza makes treaty with Bateke chief

1880s–90s European 'Scramble for Africa'

1884–85 Berlin Conference divides up continent

1885 Leopold declares the Congo Free State

1890 Anglo-German treaty allocates territory in East Africa

1905–06 Maji-maji uprising

1908–09 Watchtower movement introduced into Nyasaland by Elliot Kamwana

1915 John Chilembwe leads resistance to British rule

COLONIAL RULE

The European powers used Africa as a source of cheap raw materials to supply their industries. Many colonial governments leased vast tracts of land to private concessionary companies. It was up to these companies to exploit the natural resources of the region. Many did so through violence and forced labour.

VIOLENT OPPRESSION

One of the most brutal regimes in Central Africa was the Congo Free State, where the Belgian king Leopold II leased much of the land to concessions. The main raw material was natural rubber, obtained from tropical trees. Demand for rubber grew rapidly after 1890 because of the development of motorised vehicles and their need for tyres. Workers for the companies used all means possible to obtain rubber at the lowest prices. Armed gangs travelled up the rivers of the Congo basin to attack villages, killing and mutilating the inhabitants and taking hostages until the required amount of rubber was collected. Many Africans deserted their villages and fled away from the rivers to more remote, and often less fertile, land. African resistance and international condemnation of this system forced Leopold to hand over the Free State to the Belgian government in 1908, when some of the worst excesses of violence came to an end.

The European owner of a rubber plantation watches as his crop is weighed in 1910.

WHITE SETTLEMENT

British-run Kenya was widely settled by white people. Here, as elsewhere, the interests of the white settlers were placed before those of the local African population. In the early 20th century the British brought about 32,000 workers from India to construct a railway line from Mombasa on the coast to Lake Victoria. Thousands of these workers then settled in Kenya and Uganda and became involved in commerce. Largely to stifle competition from the Indians, white settlers demanded that large areas of fertile land in central Kenya be reserved for them alone. African farmers had also seized the opportunity to grow Arabica coffee, which was more profitable than the Robusta variety. Again, demands from white settlers led to a white-only monopoly on growing Arabica coffee.

Workers on a Kenyan coffee farm in 1953.

WORLD WAR I

World War I (1914-18) was essentially a European war fought between Germany and Austria-Hungary against Britain and its empire, France and Russia. But the war also spread to Africa. France recruited thousands of African troops to fight in Europe, while Britain and Germany fought over Tanganyika, in East Africa. It is estimated that 1 million Kenyans and Ugandans were forced to work as porters for the British army in East Africa: at least 100,000 died in this service. At the end of the war, the former German colonies were reallocated by the European victors. In Central Africa, Britain gained Tanganyika, while Belgium got Rwanda and Burundi, and Britain and France divided Cameroon between them.

The post-war period saw the start of the exploitation of Africa's mineral wealth. In the Belgian Congo, rich copper reserves were discovered in Katanga. As the region was sparsely populated, workers were recruited from many miles away. This pattern of migrant labour became a feature of colonial rule across Central Africa. Colonial governments imposed taxes on the African populations, forcing many African men to leave their homes to look for work in mines and on plantations, all owned by Europeans.

COLONIAL RULE

1901 By this date, most colonial boundaries have been agreed

1901–14 Colonial administrations established throughout region

1908 Congo Free State taken over by the Belgian government

1914–18 World War I: Britain and Germany fight over German Tanganyika; Germany loses its African colonies to Britain, France and Belgium at the end of the war

1920s Exploitation of copper reserves in Katanga, southern Congo, begins. White settlers take land from Africans in places such as Kenya and Southern Rhodesia (Zimbabwe)

1920s–30s Early growth of African nationalist movements in the region

T E ROAD TO I DEPENDENCE

During World War II (1939–45), Africa was once again drawn into a European war. The African colonies were a vital source of men and materials for Britain and France.

African colonial troops in the British Army help to build a bridge in Libya, 1943.

IMPACT OF THE WAR

The war marked a turning-point in Africa, as the rise of nationalism meant that African attitudes towards the colonial powers would never be the same again. Both Britain and France began to plan limited reforms, small and cautious steps towards eventual independence. However, it soon became clear that the colonial powers could no longer dictate the pace of change in Africa.

TANGANYIKA

One example of the power of nationalism was Tanganyika. In 1929 a discussion group called the Tanganyika African Association (TAA) established branches throughout the country. The use of the Swahili language made it possible for the many different ethnic groups to communicate freely and was an important factor in the move to independence. In 1951 the TAA led resistance to an attempted eviction of thousands of farmers to make way for white settlers. In 1954 Julius Nyerere reformed the TAA into a political party called the Tanganyika African National Union (TANU). Progress to independence was swift. In 1961 Tanganyika became independent, with Nyerere as the country's first prime minister. In 1964 Tanganyika and the island state of Zanzibar merged to form Tanzania.

ATTITUDES TO DECOLONISATION

The various colonial powers had quite different policies towards their African colonies. France tried to keep its colonies as part of a 'Greater France'. Many Africans were prepared to accept this so long as they were treated equally with French citizens. However, it soon became clear that this was not going to be the case.

In 1958 French president General Charles de Gaulle issued an ultimatum to the French African colonies. In a referendum, people could vote either yes or no to self-government under French rule. If the majority voted no, the colony would have

Julius Nyerere (1922–99), president of Tanzania.

DATES OF INDEPENDENCE

1960	Cameroon (France)
	Central African Republic (France)
	Democratic Republic of the Congo (Belgium)
	Gabon (France)
	Republic of the Congo (France)
1961	Tanganyika (Tanzania) (Britain)
1962	Burundi (Belgium)
	Rwanda (Belgium)
	Uganda (Britain)
1963	Kenya (Britain)
1964	Malawi (Britain)
	Zambia (Britain)
1968	Equatorial Guinea (Spain)
1975	Angola (Portugal)
	Mozambique (Portugal)
1980	Zimbabwe (Britain)

complete independence but all French support would be withdrawn immediately. Given such a stark choice, all the colonies except Guinea voted to maintain links with France. But continuing pressure from the remaining colonies resulted in all French colonies becoming independent in 1960.

Portugal and Belgium, meanwhile, had no plans for reform of their colonies. Belgium took drastic steps to keep the people of the Congo isolated from the move to independence in other parts of Africa (see page 24). Portugal was a poor country and it regarded its African colonies as vital for its economy. Its determination to keep its colonies led to open warfare before independence was eventually granted.

THE ROAD TO INDEPENDENCE

1929 Tanganyika African Association (TAA) formed

1939–45 World War II

1944 French leader Charles de Gaulle promises 'new deal' to people of French colonies

1945 Fifth Pan-African Congress held in Manchester, UK

1950s Mau Mau struggle in Kenya

1953 Formation of Central African Federation

1954 Nyerere reforms TAA into Tanganyika African National Union (TANU)

1958 Referendum in French colonies

1960 French West and Equatorial

African colonies become independent

1961 Tanganyika becomes independent

1964 Tanganyika and Zanzibar form Republic of Tanzania

KENYA

In general, the colonies in Central Africa that had larger populations of white settlers endured a more violent transition to independence. This was because the settlers were usually unwilling to give up control over government and land.

LAND ISSUES

In Kenya the 3,000 or so white settlers who farmed the fertile highlands (see page 19) dominated the colony and were determined to hold on to political and economic power. In the years after World War II, many squatter tenants were thrown off white farms in the highlands. In return for farming small areas of land, these squatters had provided an occasional workforce for white farmers. Increasingly, however, white farmers were using more intensive methods of agriculture and wanted to remove the squatters from their land. Many of these squatters were Kikuyu. As a result of their grievances, violent action against white-owned land and property began in the 1940s.

THE MAU MAU RISING

Nationalist sentiment increased with the founding in 1944 of the Kenyan African Union (KAU). In 1947 Jomo Kenyatta became its leader and travelled the country urging freedom from colonial rule and settler domination. In 1952 Kikuyu guerrillas, called Mau Mau by the British, began a campaign of violence. In response, the colonial government declared a state of

Approximately 2,000 Mau Mau terrorist suspects await questioning by the police, 24 October 1952.

JOMO KENYATTA

Jomo Kenyatta was born near Nairobi sometime between 1890 and 1895 (the year of his birth is not certain). He was educated at a Scottish Mission Centre and converted to Christianity in 1914. He took a great interest in Kikuyu issues; by 1925 he was one of the leaders of the Kikuyu Central Association (KCA). The KCA sent Kenyatta to Britain in 1929 to lobby for Kikuyu land rights. During the 1930s he studied in London and, briefly, in Moscow. During World War II, Kenyatta remained in Britain; he took part in the fifth Pan-African Congress in Manchester in 1945. Returning to Kenya, Kenyatta became president of the Kenyan African Union in 1947. He was arrested in 1952 and a year later imprisoned for his alleged involvement in the Mau Mau movement. He was finally freed in 1961. As the first prime minister of Kenya from 1963, Kenyatta presided over a stable and peaceful country. He died in office in 1978.

emergency and arrested African nationalist leaders, including Kenyatta, who was jailed in 1953. The Mau Mau rising was put down with great ferocity; thousands of Africans were killed. Although it did not succeed in its main aims, the Mau Mau campaign did demonstrate to the British government that the settlers' demands were excessive and that black rule was inevitable.

INDEPENDENCE

In 1959 the state of emergency was lifted. Kenyatta was freed in 1961 and became president of the recently formed Kenya African National Union (KANU). In 1963 Kenyatta led his country to independence.

Kenyatta died in office in 1978 and was succeeded by Daniel Arap Moi. Moi declared a one-party state in 1982 and suppressed opposition to his rule. When opposition leaders formed the Forum for the Restoration of Democracy (FORD) in 1990, Moi outlawed it and arrested its members. Following fierce international criticism, many countries suspended aid payments to Kenya.

By the end of 1991, a multi-party system had been reinstated. In elections held the following year, Moi was re-elected to power.

In an attempt to tackle corruption at the highest levels of government, Moi appointed the anthropologist and opposition politician Richard Leakey to head an anti-corruption drive. In 2002 nearly 40 years of KANU dominance ended when Mwai Kibaki of the National Rainbow Coalition won a victory over his KANU rival, Uhuru Kenyatta (son of Jomo). Kibaki has pledged to tackle corruption in Kenyan politics.

FACT FILE: KENYA

Colonial history: British colony
Independence: 1963
Area: 582,650 sq km
Capital: Nairobi
Official languages: Kiswahili, English
Population: 32 million (2003)
Ethnic make-up: Kikuyu 22%, Luhya 14%,
   Luo 13%, Kalenjin 12%, Kamba 11%,
   other Africans 27%, non-Africans 1%

MOZAMBIQUE

After World War II, Portugal was determined to hold on to its African colonies and treated them as overseas provinces. Emigration from Portugal was encouraged and thousands of white settlers moved to Mozambique during the 1950s. At the same time, an independence movement was gathering pace among Africans.

FACT FILE: MOZAMBIQUE

Colonial history: Portuguese colony
Independence: 1975
Area: 801,590 sq km
Capital: Maputo
Official language: Portuguese
Population: 18.8 million (2003)
Ethnic make-up: Makua Longwe 47%,
  Tsonga 23%, Malawi 12%, Shona 11%,
  Yao 4%, others 3%

FIGHT FOR INDEPENDENCE

In 1962 activists from several anti-colonial groups came together to form the Mozambique Liberation Front, known as Frelimo. Two years later, Frelimo started a war of independence against colonial rule.

Ten years of warfare led to independence in 1975, with the Frelimo leader Samora Machel as president. Machel established a single-party system, and in 1977 declared Frelimo a Marxist party. In the years that followed independence, Mozambique became drawn into the internal politics of neighbouring Southern Rhodesia and South Africa. Because Mozambique supported the struggle against white rule in Rhodesia, a group of Rhodesians developed a rebel movement within Mozambique – the Mozambique Resistance Movement (Renamo) – to try to destabilise the Frelimo government. When Rhodesia became independent as Zimbabwe in 1980, South Africa took over the backing of

Renamo in retaliation for Mozambique's support for the African National Congress (ANC). In 1982 Renamo launched attacks on schools, clinics and transport across Mozambique and the country descended into chaos and civil war.

The civil war continued throughout the 1980s, despite a shortlived ceasefire in 1984. In 1986 Machel was killed in a plane crash in South Africa; Joaquim Chissano became

Samora Machel, president of Mozambique from 1975 until his death in an air crash in 1986.

Floods devastated Mozambique in 2000 and 2001, submerging large parts of the country.

president. He ended the Marxist regime in 1989, and in 1990 amended the constitution to allow for a democratic, multi-party political system. At the same time, the apartheid regime in South Africa was coming to an end and its support for Renamo dried up. In 1992 President Chissano and the Renamo leader Afonso Dhaklama signed a peace deal to end the civil war.

A New Beginning

In democratic elections held in 1994 and 1999, Frelimo returned to power under Chissano. Support for Renamo remained strong, however, and in 2000 riots broke out as Renamo supporters protested against the election result. Chissano therefore decided to step down after his second term

ended in 2004. The Frelimo candidate, and expected victor, in the election is Armando Guebuza.

Mozambique is still recovering from the civil war that wrecked the country. The situation was made worse in 2000 and 2001 when it experienced terrible floods. The drought that followed in 2002 brought many close to famine. Mozambique's economy may be booming, with many multinational companies investing in the country, but this wealth has as yet had little or no impact on the estimated 80% of people who live in poverty in towns and rural areas.

35

ANGOLA

Like Mozambique, Angola experienced an influx of Portuguese settlers during the 1950s. It was soon clear that independence from colonial rule would not be won without a fight.

A THREE-WAY FIGHT

Three independence movements emerged in Angola to fight Portuguese rule, and each received support from different sections of the population. The Popular Movement for the Liberation of Angola (MPLA), founded in 1956 by Agostinho Neto, drew its support from the mixed African-Portuguese· population in Luanda and from the Kimbundu. The National Front for the Liberation of Angola (FNLA), set up in 1961, drew its support from the Bakongo in the north. Unita, set up by Jonas Savimbi in

Luanda, capital of Angola, is situated on one of the finest natural harbours in Africa.

FACT FILE: ANGOLA

Colonial history: Portuguese colony
Independence: 1975
Area: 1,246,700 sq km
Capital: Luanda
Official language: Portuguese
Population: 13.6 million (2003)
Ethnic make-up: Ovimbundu 37%,
   Kimbundu 25%, Bakongo 13%, others 25%

1966, was a rural movement supported by the Ovimbundu people. The three guerrilla movements fought a lengthy war until Angola finally became independent in 1975.

CIVIL WAR

With the coming of independence, a power struggle broke out between the MPLA on one side and the FNLA and Unita on the other. The situation was complicated by the interference of foreign powers. Cuba and the Soviet Union backed the MPLA, Zaire and the USA backed the FNLA, while South Africa backed Unita. With the help of Cuban troops, the MPLA expelled the FNLA and pushed Unita into the south.

The civil war continued throughout the 1980s. In 1987 South African troops invaded Angola in support of Unita. An agreement for their withdrawal, and for the withdrawal of Cuban troops, was signed by Savimbi and Jose Eduardo dos Santos (leader of the MPLA since Neto's death in 1979). But guerrilla fighting continued until 1991, when the United Nations stepped in to negotiate a peace deal. A new constitution abandoned the previous one-party system and opened the way for multi-party elections.

PEACE AT LAST

The first democratic elections held in Angola in 1992 resulted in victory for the MPLA. Savimbi rejected the outcome and Unita resumed the guerrilla war. Another peace agreement signed in 1994 heralded the arrival of UN peacekeepers the following year. But an attempt to set up a power-sharing government in 1997 failed and full-scale war broke out once again in 1998. The UN withdrew its troops in 1999.

In 2002 Savimbi was killed by government troops. His death opened up the prospect for peace. A few months later Unita rebels agreed a ceasefire. Many refugees began to

JONAS SAVIMBI

Jonas Savimbi founded Unita in 1966 and remained a key and often controversial figure in Angola until his death in 2002. He was born in 1934 in the eastern Angolan province of Moxico, a rural region that provided the main support for Unita. Savimbi was seen by some as a freedom-fighter and by others as a warmonger. Under his leadership, Unita received support from the apartheid regime in South Africa, and from the USA. In 1986, US president Ronald Reagan spoke of Unita winning 'a victory that electrifies the world and brings great sympathy and assistance from other nations to those struggling for freedom'. However, when elections in 1992 resulted in victory for the MPLA, Savimbi refused to accept the result and took the country back to war, refusing to attend negotiations for a peace deal in 1994. Savimbi was killed in 2002.

return home but after 27 years of warfare the country was in ruins and famine was a constant threat. In 2003 Unita completed its transformation from a rebel group into a political party when it elected Isaias Samakuva as its new leader. The next elections will be held in 2006.

REGIONAL ISSUES

Many of the countries in Central Africa have endured years of warfare, often civil war. The legacy of the fighting can be found everywhere. War disrupts everyday life, forcing people to flee from their homes and their livelihoods to live as refugees.

During her lifetime, Diana, Princess of Wales, campaigned for a ban on the use of landmines.

EFFECTS OF WAR

War has a devastating effect on a country's economy: infrastructure is destroyed and tourists stop visiting. In the aftermath of war, Angola and Mozambique have both faced the problem of landmines: small, lethal weapons that explode when someone steps on them or picks them up, causing death or loss of limbs. Mines are often forgotten once fighting stops.

FOOD SUPPLY

Zimbabwe was once known as the 'bread-basket of Africa' because of its rich agricultural land. Today, a mixture of disastrous political policies (see page 39) and drought have led to severe food shortages. An estimated one-third of Zimbabwe's people are now malnourished. Angola is now enjoying some stability but it cannot feed its people. During the war, many fled rural areas, leaving land untended. Now, even those who remained in the countryside cannot farm because of landmines. In Mozambique, food shortages are largely due to crop failures caused by flooding and drought in 2000-02.

AIDS

One of the biggest challenges for Africa is to bring the AIDS epidemic under control. AIDS – acquired immune deficiency syndrome – is caused by the HIV virus which attacks the body's immune system. HIV is spread from person to person through body fluids. There is no cure for AIDS and the drugs used to slow down the virus are very expensive. In many countries, AIDS has been controlled by improved health education, but in Africa millions have died. In countries where people are malnourished and where there is little health care, AIDS is rampant. But some countries, notably Uganda, have fought the disease. There the number of adults suffering from AIDS has dropped from 14% in the early 1990s to 5% in 2003. This has been achieved through a widespread education programme.

THE FUTURE

'The state of Africa is a scar on the conscience of the world.' These words, spoken by British Prime Minister Tony Blair in 2001, sum up the desperate situation in many Central African countries. In most cases, these nations are defined by artificial borders laid down more than 100 years ago by land-hungry white men in faraway Europe. In the Democratic Republic of the Congo, continued fighting sent waves of refugees into neighbouring Burundi in 2004, causing problems for the fragile peace in that country. The political situation in Zimbabwe continues to worsen, while in Uganda rebels in the north of the country have caused 1.5 million people to flee their homes. Despite hopeful signs for the future in some Central African countries, it is clear that, within the entire region, many flashpoints remain.

Uganda has succeeded in dramatically reducing HIV/AIDS infection rates by increasing health education.

GLOSSARY

African National Congress (ANC) Main black opposition organisation in South Africa during apartheid. The ANC was banned in 1961 and began a campaign of resistance against white rule; the ban was lifted in 1990. Today the ANC is the main political party in South Africa.

Amputee Someone who has had a limb (arm or leg) or limbs removed.

Apartheid Policy of racial discrimination developed in South Africa which gave power to the white minority and excluded the black majority; the system ended by 1994.

Bantu Name given to a family of over 500 languages spoken throughout West and Central Africa.

Cassava Food plant grown in tropical regions. It has fleshy roots that are poisonous when raw but can be processed into a variety of products.

Commonwealth of Nations Association of countries once ruled by Britain.

Concession Grant of rights over land given by a government to a commercial or trading company.

Constitution Political principles on which a country is governed, often written down in a single document.

Constitutional monarchy Country with a king or queen at its head, where the powers of the monarch are limited and defined by the constitution.

Coup Sudden seizure of power over the government of a country.

Democracy System of government in which the people of a country have a direct say in how their country is run, usually through elected representatives.

Dictator Absolute ruler not restricted by a country's constitution or laws.

Ethnic Relating to a group of people who share similar racial characteristics.

Evangelical Christians Christians for whom conversion to the Christian faith is an important part of their belief.

Genocide Deliberate killing of one nationality or ethnic group by another.

Guerrilla Member of an irregular armed force set up to fight regular forces such as the army or police.

Lobby To influence politicians and those in power by persuasion and argument.

Marxist Political and economic philosophy based on the writings of the German thinker Karl Marx, who founded communism.

Migrant labour Practice of travelling away from home in order to find work.

Millet Small-grained cereal crop grown in tropical and semi-tropical regions.

Multi-party politics Political system in which different political parties compete for power.

Mutiny Open rebellion against government or military authority.

Nationalism Loyalty to one's country; in colonial times, a belief in the right of a country to obtain independence.

Pastoralism Way of life characterised by the keeping of herds of animals.

Power Nation that has great influence over international affairs.

Power-sharing government Political system in which power is held by government and opposition representatives working together.

Raffia Fibre made from the leaves of the raffia palm, native to Africa.

Referendum Direct vote by the people of a country on a particular issue.

Regime System of government of a particular political party.

Savannah Grassland regions in the tropics and subtropics.

Socialism Political and economic theory in which land, factories and other means of production are held under public rather than private ownership.

Sorghum Cereal crop grown as a staple food in Africa and Asia.

United Nations (UN) International peacekeeping organisation, founded in 1945 and based in New York.

War crimes tribunal Special international court that meets to examine accusations of crimes committed during wartime.

Yam Food plant grown in the tropics and sub-tropics which produces large tubers.

INDEX